AF413631

ALL ABOUT BANKS

Finance Bank for Kids

Children's Money & Saving Reference

Speedy Publishing LLC

40 E. Main St. #1156

Newark, DE 19711

www.speedypublishing.com

Copyright 2017

Banks are business that accept and hold money for customers. In return for holding this money, they pay interest. They make money from making loans to other people and businesses at a higher interest rate. In this book, you will be learning more about the business of banking.

BANK

WHY ARE BANKS IMPORTANT TO THE ECONOMY?

Banks help with the flow of money for business to occur. They keep your savings safe, but use this money in helping others to purchase cars, houses, and to start a business. This makes banks essential to modern economy.

A BOY DEPOSITING HIS MONEY IN A BANK

WHAT IS A DEPOSIT?

One of the essential functions of a bank is accepting and holding deposits. This is money that customers put into the bank. There are two types of accounts that customers utilize:

Savings Account – This account is mostly used for saving money. They provide less services and access than the checking account, but usually offer a higher interest rate and charge less fees.

Checking Account – This is an account where a person has easy access to their money. A customer can write a check or use a debit card to access their money deposited into a checking account.

Often there are fees that are associated with the checking account, and the account might have a minimum balance requirement.

Certificate of Deposit

Some of the other types of accounts provided by banks include Money Market Accounts, Certificate of Deposits (CDs), and Individual Retirement Accounts.

WHAT ARE TRANSACTIONS?

Depositing money into and out of your bank account is known as a transaction. There are several ways to add money to your account or take money out. Going to the bank in person to deposit money or take money out is probably the most obvious way. Some additional ways include:

- Check
- ATM
- Debit Card
- Electronic Transactions

MAN WITHDRAWING MONEY FROM ATM

YOUR NAME
YOUR ADDRESS HERE
DATE
PAY TO THE
ORDER OF
$
FOR
5678

Check – Writing a check is one of the oldest ways to access money in your checking account. Once you write a check for a certain value and you then sign the check, the business or person to who it is made out it can go to the bank and obtain the funds.

ATM (Automated Teller Machine) - Banks typically offer a card that can be used at ATMs which are located in different places such as a gas station or grocery store.

With the card and your password, the ATM will provide you cash and then deduct it from your account. ATMs can also be found at banks, so you do not have to go inside the bank.

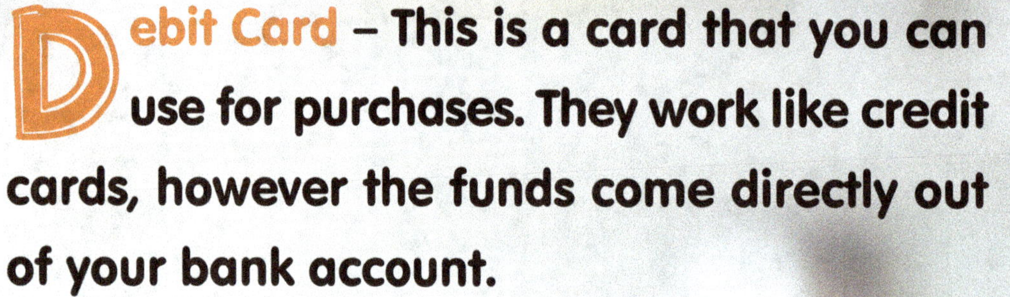

Debit Card – This is a card that you can use for purchases. They work like credit cards, however the funds come directly out of your bank account.

YOUNG WOMAN PAYING BY
DEDIT CARD AT JUICE BAR

TRANSACTION

Electronic Transactions – You can also move money in and out of your bank account electronically. Direct deposit is one such instance of an electronic transaction, where your paycheck is forwarded directly to your bank account. The money is electronically forwarded from your employer's account directly to your checking account.

LOANS

anks utilize the money that is deposited for loans for other people as well as businesses. They charge an interest rate for these loans that is higher than the rate they pay for deposits to make money. People borrow money from banks for purchasing homes (mortgage), cars, and for starting businesses.

RECEIVING THE BORROWED
MONEY FROM A BANK

FEDERAL DEPOSIT INSURANCE CORPORATIO
BUILDING IN ARLINGTON, VA
FEDERAL DEPOSIT INSURANCE CORPORATION

Even if a bank is robbed or goes out of business, your money is safe. Up to a specific amount, most deposits are protected by the government under the FDIC (Federal Deposit Insurance Corporation).

HOW DO I MANAGE MY CHECKBOOK?

nce you open a checking account with the bank, you will receive a checkbook that contains a checkbook register, deposit slips, and checks.

THE CHECKS

Typically, when you are opening a new checking account, the person assisting you at the bank will provide you with a checkbook that contains a few new checks. You will want to order additional checks from the bank or any other check-printing company.

You can choose checks from all sorts of designs if you want to. They contain various backgrounds, including animals, the beach, or even your favorite sports team.

SIGNING A CHECK

THE REGISTER

You will also find a register inside the checkbook. This is used to record all events, such as recording a check that you have written, any withdrawals of cash, and any deposits. It is very important that you record each transaction so that you will always know how much money is in your checking account.

If you happen to miss a transaction, you might end up writing another check or withdrawing more money than you have available in the account, and the bank will typically charge you a fine when this happens.

BALANCING YOUR CHECKBOOK

You should receive a statement from your bank each month. You will want to review both to ensure that they match. This is referred to as balancing your checkbook. If they do not match, you will need to review each item to make sure that everything is correct.

190.55
191
32.76
12.85
36.15
135.14
1200.00
25.98
100.00
BALANCE
B/Forward
CREDIT
DEBIT
Note - cheques etc., are accepted subject
to examination and verification and are
transmitted for collection at customer's risk.
Though credited to account when paid in,
they should not be drawn against until
cleared.
rd

DEPOSIT SLIP.
NAME:
DATE:
Deposits are governe...
agreement and may not be...
ACCOUNT NUMBER:

DEPOSIT SLIPS

You will also find deposit slips inside your new checkbook, which are used for depositing money into the bank. In order to make your trip to the bank faster, you will want to fill out the deposit slip before you go. If you have run out of deposit slips, they will have some at the bank that you can use, however, they do not contain your account information like the slips contained in your checkbook.

WHAT HAPPENS ONCE I WRITE A CHECK?

Banks and stores are able to process checks quite fast, and sometimes the funds may be taken out of the account on the same day that you have written the check. The store then sends these checks to their local bank at the end of the day.

The check's value is encoded into numbers which can be found at the bottom of the check. The check is then processed through a fast sorter/reader and the information is forwarded to the Federal Reserve clearinghouse electronically. At this point, your bank is able to see and pay the amount to the payee.

HOW TO SAVE MONEY

What should you do with money you receive for doing a chore or received as a gift or allowance? You have two options here: spend it or save it. While spending your money right away might seem to be the most fun, saving it can be enjoyable as well.

WHY SHOULD I SAVE MY MONEY?

There are several reasons you might want to save it rather than spending it right away. Here is a list of just a few ideas:

- **To buy something big** – If you save your money over time, you can build your savings to buy a bicycle, a video game console you want, or even start saving now to buy that car you want someday.

- **To have cash available on hand** – You might want to have some cash available for that time when something you want to do comes up. Perhaps, going with your friends to see a movie that was just released.

● **Emergencies** – Occasionally, emergencies happen, such as needing to replace your cell phone that quit working.

BANK
vs

REAL BANK OR PIGGY BANK

Where should you keep the money you are saving? While you could keep it in your house somewhere safe such as your wallet, a piggy bank, or with your parents, you also might choose to put some of it in the bank. Many banks have special accounts provided just to kids and these accounts sometimes earn interest. Not only are you saving your money, but you are also adding more to it.

INTEREST

If you are saving your money at the bank, the bank just might actually pay you for your money. This is referred to as interest. Typically, this interest is compounded monthly, which means that they pay interest on your account each month. While it may seem a small amount, such as 1%, it is better than what your money would make at home in the piggy bank.

nterest
rate

Interest can add up over time. If you have $1,000 in your account for 10 years at a rate of 3% interest, you would have made $349.35 in interest during that 10 years, which is a decent amount of money for doing nothing.

nterest is a great reason to start saving early and can help you save for those big items that happen later in life such as buying a car or going off to college.

HOW TO HELP YOUR FAMILY SAVE

There are ways that you can help your family save money. Listed below are some ideas on how you can help in lowering costs around the house:

- When you leave a room, turn off the light. This saves money by using less power.
- Instead of sodas, drink water. Water is healthier for you.

- When purchasing clothes, look for items that are on sale.
- Help your parents locate coupons in the newspaper or online.

- **Discuss saving money with your parents. Ask them how you can help.**
- **Think about other ways that you can help your family when it comes to saving money.**

LEARN NOW HOW TO SAVE MONEY

Learning to save money now can be an important skill to have later in life. Being able to put some money away rather than spending it all will keep you from getting into debt as an adult.

It is important to learn about banking when you are young so that you learn at an early age how to maintain your checkbook as well as how to save money.

BANK

For additional information about banks, you can visit your local library, research the internet, and ask questions, of your teachers, family, and friends. You might even want to ask your parents to take you to the bank.

Visit
BABY PROFESSOR
EDUCATION KIDS
www.BabyProfessorBooks.com
to download Free Baby Professor eBooks
and view our catalog of new and exciting
Children's Books